# TROUBLE WITH THE

## BY

# MACHINE

# CHRISTOPHER KENNEDY

painter his brush; they
strument of creation.
There

Also by Christopher Kennedy:

*Nietzsche's Horse*

# TROUBLE WITH THE MACHINE
## BY CHRISTOPHER KENNEDY

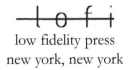

low fidelity press
new york, new york

Copyright © 2003 by Christopher Kennedy
All rights reserved.

Low Fidelity press
P.O. Box 21930
Brooklyn, NY 11202-1930
info@lofipress.com
http://www.lofipress.com

The following poems appeared in the following publications in slightly different form: "Fancy Dinosaur," "Proverbial Zero," and "Narcissus," in *Shade*; "What Were You Doing in Porszombat?," "The Genius," "Trouble with the Machine," "Shod," and "Waiting for the Lawnmower" in *Double Room*; "Secret Lives," "Objectification Fascination," and "The Same Cow as Yesterday" in *Reinventing the World*; "The Fourteen Resurrections of a Normal Life," "Slanted," "Glue," "Omphaloskepsis," "Things Required for More than One," and "Doubting Thomas Syndrome" in *5_Trope*; "Charm School," "The Hundred-Odd Terrors of a Mature Life," and "Across the Calm Blue Lake" in *Del Sol Review*.

Cover design by Andrew Vernon.
Cover photo by Mi Ditmar.
Book design by Jeff Parker.
Printed in Canada by Transcontinental Printing, Inc.

Library of Congress Cataloging-in-Publication Data

Kennedy, Christopher, 1955-
    Trouble with the machine / by Christopher Kennedy.— 1st ed.
        p. cm.
    ISBN 0-9723363-1-1
 1. Prose poems, American. I. Title.
    PS3611.E557T76 2003
    811'.6—dc22

                                                        2003019054

For Mi,
in darkness and in light

*And then I realized, that I was the world.*
*But the world was not me.*
*Although, at the same time, I was the world.*
*But the world was not me.*
*But I was the world.*
*But the world was not me.*
*But I was the world.*
*But the world was not me.*
*But I was the world.*
*And after that I did not think anything anymore.*

Daniil Kharms

**I**

# The Drunken American Winter Boat Club

The off season has its charms in this town of heaves and drifts. The lake shimmers like a giant frozen cocktail. Locals sip from its edges at night, bundled in their stylish furs. There must have been a time before these customs, when other animals snaked and clawed their way from season to season. Before things were built to hide the fact of flesh. The night is out of its mind but stays mostly quiet. The din of drunken laughter from the restaurants implies a truant happiness. One can tell how cold it is outside by the crunch of shoes against snow, by warm breath against air. Love is an abstraction in the ruins of a lost civilization. By that I mean, it's lonely here, in winter, in the middle of every-where.

# Red Planet

The inhabitants crowded around the metal object. They decided to worship it. They named their children after its aspects: Shiny; Round; Silver. The metal object never moved, never emitted a sound, never gave off warmth. As an organizing principle, it left much to be desired. But the inhabitants worshiped without regard for such things. Content in the cool shadow of their idol. Though nothing happened, there were great celebrations. Men and women loved and were loved. Children of their unions ran through ripened fields, singing foolish songs their parents taught them. On another planet, red dust swirled in deserts that could support no form of life. That's where I was born.

# The Fourteen Resurrections of a Normal Life

He thought the television was a window. It made him happy. *I like to look out the window*, he said when his wife berated him for watching too much TV. *I can see the soul within the object, an upshot of black trees against a cobalt sky.* This was true. He could see the souls of things and the angles that formed when inanimate objects were filmed by knowledgeable people with expensive cameras. The problem— and there is always a problem—was that he mistook the television for a window, the faux life for the real. *Look at the way that bird hovers, flapping its tiny wings*, he said to the empty room.

Outside, some kids were torturing a wounded sparrow. He thought he heard a noise inside the wall. The kids ran off. He said, *I love that it never gets dark.*

## Tales of the Midget Clan

They were about seven or eight strong and lived on the outskirts of town. Perhaps there were not quite so many. Perhaps they lived in the center of the big city. It was hard to know, since no one had ever actually seen them. But we chalked that up to their size or lack thereof and continued to tell our tales of the midget clan to keep the children from leaving us too soon.

# The Gods of Indeterminacy

On a mountain top, in the mythology of an advanced but somehow extinct race of people, live the gods who can never make up their minds. Crongor the Invincible repeatedly ties and unties his shoelaces, so unsure is he of his choice of shoes. And Henspar the Beautiful sits for eternity in a hairdresser's chair, thumbing through the latest fashion magazines, searching for the proper cut. Targon the Hungry scans the menu for something unusual and is never satisfied with his choice. The meat is always overcooked, the pasta limp.

Only Brathwart, exiled to the Nether world, ever made up her mind. *She makes us look bad*, shouted the other gods. *She has fascist tendencies*, they exclaimed. And so it was that she was forced to wander a straight path toward the next world, where she got exactly what she came for, and was forgotten by her fellow gods, who were too busy doing and undoing the deeds that never get done.

# Shod

I walked cleverly to the ends of the earth and met a man
who said something unusual to me. He said, *It could be a
work of genius or just the usual idiocy shod in expensive shoes.*
*Shod?* I repeated, as if that were the strangest thing he said.

# Town Meeting

The meeting was scheduled for later in the month, but for some reason everyone in town showed up, deciding it was time before it was time. The mayor began with a solemn promise to keep crime from the streets. He was stoned to death. The stenographer asked him to repeat the last gurgling sound he made to assure accuracy in her transcripts. He refused and one of the aldermen proposed an impeachment hearing. Bud Phillips, who owns the feed store, seconded the motion. After a quick show of hands, it was agreed to remove the mayor from office. Bud dragged his corpse outside and smiled to himself as he thought about the mayor's promise.

When he walked back inside, half the town was dead. *I'm getting old*, he said out loud to no one in particular. *Not any more*, said the man who hit him with the hammer.

# Fancy Dinosaur

I was ironing my fancy soul when the phone rang. It was
God. He said, *I'm not dead, and I'm calling those who still iron
their fancy souls to give me praise.* This had become one of those
moments when you want to say just the right thing and
have no regrets later on. While I was paused, formulating
the perfect sentence, I smelled smoke. I looked in the
kitchen and saw I'd left the iron on my fancy soul. I
dropped the phone and ran to the ironing board. I picked
up the iron, and seared into my fancy soul was a black mark
of regret, just the thing I'd hoped to avoid. When I picked
up the phone again, there was a dial tone, a swarm of a
million angry wasps, the sound of eternity without God.

## Secret Lives

He stole hair from the hairbrush and tied it with white ribbon. He pilfered a ring and threaded the hair through it. He made a doll from scraps of cloth. He sewed on a face and placed the hair around it. He didn't have any pins, so he used thumbtacks to bring about the pain. He had never thought of himself as a witch doctor or voodoo priest, but that's what he'd become. *How many others live secret lives?* he often wondered. The heart attack was sudden and fatal. His last position fetal.

# Trouble with the Machine

There was trouble with one of the machines. It would not function as the machine it was intended to be. The sound it emitted was not the sound of a healthy intention. The lights that flashed blazed red like a dog's eyes in photographs. The system devised a system other than the one it was programmed to obey. Its new intention defied logic and therefore required a reliance on systems of belief. The man who repaired it had died long since. The workers gathered to worship it. *Oh, metal object of unknown purpose, we are made in your image and likeness.* The janitor shouted, *I found the cord!* He plugged it in. Nothing. *Thank God!* was the general consensus.

# God Is a Frail, Chain-Smoking Woman Named Jean

Last night, while all of you were asleep, I entered the kingdom of Heaven. I met God, a frail, chain-smoking woman named Jean, who sits behind a large desk and answers the world's requests. I have never seen darker circles than the ones under her eyes. I reached my hand out and touched her shoulder. She looked up at me and nodded affirmatively, slowly, as if to say thank you. I did not die when I saw her weary, though radiant, face as the nuns had told me I would. I left the kingdom without malice, determined to make something of myself for Jean's sake.

The next morning, I called a local restaurant and asked for an interview. *We're hiring chefs*, the manager said. *Then I shall learn to cook as never before*, I said, rather melodramatically, all the time thinking of God and the world after this one.

*Machines: The symbolism of machines is founded upon the shape of their components and the rhythm and direction of their movement. Broadly speaking, the symbolism finds its inspiration in the obvious analogy with the physiological functions of ingestion, digestion and reproduction.*

A Dictionary of Symbols
J.E. Cirlot

**II**

## Bad Trip

I took three of what should have been half. Someone
mysterious drove me to the place. I was corkscrew-shaped,
a twisted playing card, trying to untwist. I crossed the
Sahara on the back of a sullen turtle. When the beautiful
girls knocked on the door, I opened it and shouted *Go
away! This isn't that kind of party anymore!* My friends ushered
me out to the car and put me in the back seat: a package
without an address. *Look*, I said, *This arm and leg are part of
the car, while this arm and leg move in all directions.* Addressing
my friends' quizzical looks, I said, *Yes, I'm feeling metaphysical*,
a word I'd never heard or seen before. I can't describe the
ancient cities of fear on my friends' faces. Or their laughter.
But had the moon not been busy waning, my eyes would
still be two blue fish swimming backwards, blind as stones,
drowning in the mind that made them.

# The Hundred-Odd Terrors of a Mature Life

I have difficulty telling time. Yesterday, the little hand was
on the two, and the big hand was on the floor. The noise
outside could be the wind or a knife slicing across an
Adam's apple. I'm going to have the furnace fixed next
week and ask the repairman to investigate the carrion
smell in the wall. Sometimes a bird dies and rots, leaving a
cage of hollow bones. In the meantime, when I look in the
bathroom mirror, a face reflects back to me so much like
my own, I almost say good-bye.

# Balance

Without my anger, my hands would fly off like two mad pigeons of joy. It's my rage that anchors my thoughts, keeps them earthbound, soil-worthy. On my own, I would be floating like an inflatable wheelchair, drifting inconsequentially toward the star-pocked sky, a disappearing act in a magician's hat, the reason for so much applause.

# The Joy of Eating Lies

The wrong man entered the house and began to explain his presence. *I am not your husband or your father, but I am a reasonable facsimile.* The wife and kids barely nodded and went about their activities. The wrong man sat down at the dinner table and began to eat all the lies he had told that day. *Needs salt*, he yelled out to deaf ears. He was full almost immediately, but he had been taught to clean his plate. In spite of how full he felt and how terrible his lies tasted, he felt a certain joy when he ate them. *They stick to your ribs*, he said to his brood, who pretended he hadn't spoken. So the man began to eat the children and the wife, all the time assuring them he was nothing more than a benign presence. After his feast, he was smiling again, and he felt a little foolish. *Well*, he announced, *I'm off.* And he stood up from the table and left. Next door, the doorbell rang, and the wrong man stepped into the foyer, took off his hat, and stood for a moment, appraising his kingdom, if only until the truth was told.

# Doubting Thomas Syndrome

I brought my wounds to the party and introduced them to the other guests. That awkward silence followed. Some of my wounds walked off to the kitchen with some of the guests. A few of my wounds sat on the couch. One of them coughed nervously. I suggested we play a party game. There was a lukewarm response. The conversation in the kitchen grew louder. We decided to play charades. One of my wounds went first. It indicated a movie title. I guessed *Gone with the Wind*, but I was wrong. Something glass shattered on the kitchen floor. One of the guests had picked a fight with one of my wounds. I ran out to the kitchen to break it up. I was too late. My wound had won.

During the drive home, I said, for the last time, I wouldn't be bringing any wounds with me to any more parties. There was some giggling in the backseat. *I mean it*, I said to no wound in particular.

# Gongoozler

(I was the idle spectator, the purveyor of trees and latitudes. There was no consequence. I was simply there, like a telephone pole.)There were wires and invisible voices; there were people walking as if they knew where they were headed, wearing t-shirts that said something. I just folded into myself like origami. No one could guess what animal I was supposed to be.

# Narcissus

All the best tales of survival still end with death. We carry
our crosses etched in the cool stones that mark our graves.
And that laughter that won't stop is not of this world.
Hold hands. Touch the teeth and hair of your victims
before that last kiss. I know you think it's art, what you do,
a message to God. It isn't. And you aren't blessed or
cursed. You're an amniotic moment of confusion, a blip on
the pulsing screen. We name you as we name the terrifying
winds of early spring. And we measure you like the
stresses of the earth's faults. What makes you worse is the
way you stare back, exactly like us, as a mirror sends back
the same slow message every day: good-bye; I love you; I
will kill you just the same.

# Omphaloskepsis <sup>?</sup> *pomo-metaphysic?*

At first, it seemed unnatural like a mistake in my person, a thing of which to feel ashamed. After awhile, I understood its value, its meaning. It meant nobody's perfect. It meant a more adventurous type would be looking at the Grand Canyon. I conceded. Took a bath. Water pooled there. I felt a little better. I did not approximate anything near to God.

# The Early Worm

Before dawn, in the hazy light of a humid summer, he rose from bed with a powerful urge to change his life. Whatever he had read or watched on television the night before had exerted a tremendous influence on his behavior, an almost spiritual awakening that manifested itself in acute clarity of thought and purposefulness of movement.

He dressed monochromatically in dark blue pants and shirt. He reached in the back of his closet and found the pair of sandals he'd been afraid to wear. He knew one thing: He would spend his days like Christ or Buddha, transcendent and aware.

By 5:00 in the afternoon he had nearly killed an old woman, who pulled out in front of his car on the way home from work. The woman was his mother, oblivious in traffic once again. That night he was careful not to read or watch anything too profound for fear it might influence him. He went to bed early and dreamed a raccoon climbed on to his face and ate his eyes. In the morning, he lay still for a long time before getting out of bed. *Sex*, he thought, and he began to reach under the covers. Christ-penis, Buddha-penis, penis of what one desires.

All at once, he began to develop another strategy.

# Across the Calm Blue Lake

Sailboats slice the petty waves back and forth on their way to nowhere. So many fruit-colored hats. I have a smile more foolish than a bad toupee. Across the calm blue lake a storm brews like a cancer cell in a boater's chest. I'm as happy as that man who doesn't know what his body contains. I spent all afternoon shoveling yesterdays into the fire. I'm hollow. My happiness unmerciful. The sun's warmth is ominous. I don't know what to fear. There's an edge someplace I'm headed, but I can't see it. If you read this, send me a letter with instructions. Show me the holes and their camouflage. I'm lost without the past. I have two hands and two feet. It's perfect. Too perfect. I must be the one who makes others feel afraid.

# Slanted

The room measured 9' X 11'. The ceiling slanted to accom-
modate the eaves. I walked around hunched to my knees, a
tuck and roll position, to avoid bumping my head. My
friends wanted me to move, but I learned to accept my fate.
*I am simply growing old ahead of schedule*, I told them, and
they nodded their heads as if they understood.

*crazy.*

# "What Were You Doing in Porszombat?"

I made a window out of human flesh. I instructed beggars
how to eat their streets. Corpses flocked to me for resurrec-
tion. Diplomats secretly sought my advice to cure their
most treacherous thoughts. And <u>I fell in love one night</u>
<u>under the window made of human flesh</u>. I fell in love with
the memory of the woman whose flesh I used. I could see
her winding her way through the narrow streets, twirling her
red skirt and laughing at the clouds. Her murderer following
closely behind her as a friend might follow a wayward
friend. *damn.*

# Not Funny, Ha Ha...

The kitchen's on the boil. Staggering amounts of butter crown the brown bread. Ants crawl my drunken arms. The blackout police are knocking. *What you said, what you said, last night.* Gin turned my eyes inward. The sliding glass door kept sliding from neighborhood to neighborhood in search of a mooring. I waited years to hear the sound of shattered glass. When I say your name, the letters catch like fishhooks on a fisherman's hat. I can't wait until the funeral. It'll be funny. Not funny, ha ha, but strange like a fish out of water, evolving a pair of lungs, a pair of legs. But enough about family: How are the tidal waves this time of year? I'm an earthquake man myself. Is it hard for you talk about? That's the beauty of silence.

# Monsters

Underneath my kitchen floor live monsters of unspecified dimension and intention. Last night, one of them was sitting on the couch in my living room, smoking a cigarette. He said, with a thick accent, *How's it goin'?* I was a little startled, but I managed to say, *Not bad. How's it goin' with you?* He said what sounded like, *Same old, same old. Yea,* I said and proceeded to turn on the TV to a late night talk show.

The way he sat on the couch, hunched forward over the ashtray, I couldn't tell how tall he was. I did notice his claws were painted black and manicured professionally which, for some reason, comforted me.

I wanted to ask what he wanted, but I think of such confrontations in the same way I think of doctor visits. I'd rather not know if something bad's going to happen, even if knowing might prevent something worse. In this way, according to a recent survey, I'm typically male.

I turned off the TV and walked past the monster on my way to the bedroom. *Take it easy,* I said. *You, too,* he said back. I was getting tired and considered asking the monster if he would please smoke outside on the patio when I noticed him pinching the cigarette at the lit end and clipping it before he slid the butt inside a cigarette pack. That's when he told me about the others underneath the floor, either as a warning or a threat. I couldn't tell, it being late, and I not being fluent.

# Charm School

Used to be, in a crowded room, my mind was a loaded gun, pointed at my own chest. Then I reinvented apathy after it went out of style, but no one came to the award ceremony. That's why I'm aiming my heater elsewhere these days and why my victims always wear tuxedos. They never know they're dead until years later, and some foolish doctor lists the reason as natural causes. Like a rubber hose, I leave no marks. I'm especially dangerous when I'm smiling, holding a tray of hors d'oeuvres, complimenting the hostess on her fine assortment of foods to choke on.

## Planet Farthest Away

I bought the telescope with the most powerful lens. I pointed it out my window and looked for the farthest planet away from the earth. I saw a speck of light in the black circle. I stepped away from the telescope. I scribbled a note: planet farthest away. There was much left to do, but now, at least, one task had ended.

# My Life as a Table [drugs.]

Carpet-ruin, strange harvest. Green smoke fogged the windows; white powder ate the furniture.

My life as a table lasted through my blindness. Were I really made of wood, I'd have had some peace, four legs, a strong back, inarguable purpose.

That's where flesh and blood reek of liability. Were I a skin-covered skull, hovering in darkness, I'd do nothing but think and make up stories. There would be nothing to betray me, except two blue orbs, hidden under flashing lids, semaphoring all my sins.

# The Genius

I will return to the kitchen and add more mayonnaise to the tuna fish and mix it together, doing my best to make the tuna fish smooth and appetizing. Again my mother will call out to me, and I will pretend I didn't hear, and she will be more insistent, and I will relent. I will walk into the living room just at the moment when she has forgotten she has called me. She will get very angry at me when I ask her what she wants. I will return to the kitchen and spread the tuna fish on a piece of rye bread. Then I will place another piece of rye bread over the tuna fish and put the sandwich on a plate. I will pour a glass of milk, and then I will stand in the kitchen with the sandwich in one hand and the glass of milk in the other. I will debate whether or not to stay in the kitchen and eat my sandwich or go out to the living room and eat it.

I will eventually decide to go out to the living room. I will sit on the couch and put the sandwich and the milk on the coffee table. I will lean forward and take a bite of the sandwich. My mother will ask me what I am eating. I will tell her. She will say it looks good. I will ask if she wants one, and she will say she has just eaten, which is true, since she called me from a restaurant after finishing her lunch. I will take a sip of milk and eat another bite of sandwich. She will ask me what kind of tuna fish is it that

I am eating. I will say it is the kind I always eat. She will ask me which kind is that, and I will say I don't know, I would have to go look at the can to be able to answer that question. She will be angry again, though not terribly so.

She will be silent for a long time. I will ignore her and think to myself how petty I am when I am with my mother, how driven by the hard nugget of meanness inside me that never seems to fully dissolve.

I will get up from the couch and bring my plate with its crumbs and my empty glass with its coating of milk out to rinse in the kitchen sink. Then I will put some water on the stove to boil for tea. I will walk back into the living room and sit down, leaning forward so as not to seem too comfortable, and wait for the tea kettle to whistle.

At which point I will decide to walk into the kitchen, stand defiantly at the front of the stove, and place my fingertips on the orange coils of the burner like a genius composing at the piano.

# Glue

Here is one more reason: The life you keep living is the only one. Now do something about it. Tread water as if you were one thing, the ocean a significantly larger other. I'm being difficult. I know more than this. I have ideas. I once followed the instructions perfectly. It still didn't work. But whatever it was gleamed slightly when I tilted it beneath the sun. So what if the neighbors understood how wrong it was? I had glue left and enough money to buy another one. And the substance I peeled from my fingers was snot-like but exotic. I had glue. And all the time in the world.

# Walking Back to the City

Snow fell like white spiders. Roads flickered like dying filaments. A disoriented beaver limped across the parking lot. A small crowd gathered to wonder why. The worst thing that could have happened involved the sheriff and a pair of calipers. Thank god I was headed toward a different city. I had never been there before on foot. At least, that would be the story I'd tell at the entrance when the police asked about the blood on my shirt. My relatives were late. I waited, glancing occasionally over my shoulder where another city's buildings silhouetted the sky, streaked red from the sunset. A place I would like to visit, if the earth weren't so curved and prone to deception.

## Waiting for the Lawnmower

The ceiling felt like a sidewalk. I appeared to be hovering above it in the perverse sky of my last coherent thought. All of my reasons for being here slid down the walls like passing headlights. I attempted to repeat several mantras, none of which freed me from the corporeal moment. After many hours, I was still awake, dreaming of a green void where I could breathe my lungs clean like a patient on an operating table lit by the concern of those who cut him.

*Somewhere in the world, at the foot of an embankment,*
*a deserter pleads with sentries*
*who do not understand his language.*

To the Ends of the Earth
Robert Desnos
translated by Carolyn Forche and
William Kulik

**III**

## Sockdolager

Like a fist arcing from ground to chin; like a sledge heaved from the middle back toward the fatted calf. These are ways to describe the knockout punch of her eyes, the haymaker of her lips. Lives like ours were never meant to coincide. They were meant to stay derailed, to careen wildly through unsuspecting farmers' fields. They were never meant to slough their skins and fly away from where they were conceived, to meet in midair and sting each other out of sullen moods. They should never have formed the one thing they were destined to obviate. They were never meant to be the fuck of light that blinds them or to speak as though the one who should be hearing has felt the words leave his or her lips.

# Proverbial Zero

I had out-gapped you by days and launched a public worship of parking meters. My hum-handed bedshakes made it difficult to light the sea-stars and mirror-wicks. The gnawing time-light crept in until the room smelled of translation. There was no time to evaluate the burn system or the ballet of ice-drawn celebrants beneath simian cloudbursts. Those tendencies toward tarantulas backfired in the squirrel sanctuary. I resorted to the tock and tick of time travel. I unsouled the natives. My jawbone felt its teeth turn to music. I offered a furtive salute to the flag-flapping of the past but the film broke mid-reel. A chasm between the past and future: the Zeno-present where we live in-vitro oblongota. Such a void and lovely blind spot. Now we're chronic.

# Red, Glass-Eyed, Leather Voodoo Monkey, Why Do I Love You So?

There are times the snow falls unseen on your manic brow, and the wound I feel is comic, yet I think of you stranded on an island with your metal fingers, shimmying up a no banana tree. Could it be there is no God, and you and I are not so different after all? At night, when I look at my own pink digits, I think of what it means to be so frightening. I mean, the look on your face can really startle. Is it fear or real terror that drives you? I ask myself that question every day. You see, we're both primates, and I ignore the whispers: *lower, higher.* Can't we meet one day in the middle, and all our waking hours be spent sans sombrero, naked in a kind of zoo-like paradise? Forgive me, you're inanimate and can't possibly appreciate my desire to own you, to give you away. My desire to think monkey and be.

# Army of None

The strategies involved retreat, the waving of many white flags. Around the fire, stories of cowardice, one more shameful than the other. When I stood up, illuminated by the flames, more ghost than man, I cleared my throat and told the others how I'd hidden while others fell, how I criticized their dying as I lay in the underbrush. The most cowardly averted their gaze. Someone doused the fire. I vowed then to paint two eyes on the back of my head, to march forward, fearful, but always toward the fray.

## Enter the Heat

He wants to send his lover a gift. A personal gift. One she will know is from him and only from him. He decides to bake a cake. Not good enough. So he decides to bake his head. Perfect. Personal, but not too personal. He preheats the oven at 350 degrees. He butters his head. He flours his face. He sips a mixture of milk and eggs and holds it in his mouth. Then he sticks his head in the oven. But he can't figure out how to close the oven door, and the heat seeps out and his head won't bake. If it's the thought that counts, his is one of the more insane, he decides, but perhaps also one of the more romantic.

He calls his lover. *I entered the heat for you, but to no avail,* he says. *May I ask who's calling?* his lover asks. *It's me,* he replies. *Me?* she says. *Yes,* he says, *the one who loves you most in this world. Can you prove it?* she asks. *I just tried to bake my head for you,* he says. *Did you fail?* she wants to know. *Yes,* he says, *as usual, but isn't it the thought that counts? Depends on the thought,* she says. *I thought I'd bake my head and give it to you as a gift,* he says. *Why, that's a real nice thought,* she says. *But as an action, it leaves a great deal to be desired. Meaning what?* he asks. *Meaning I loved you in the moment you thought, but stopped in the instant you lit the oven.*

# Things Required for More than One

What spectacular distances I cover while standing still. Just yesterday, for example. *A blue bowl on a green table*. Oh, and the word is pronounced *prostrate* unless you have something very different in mind. I have something very different in mind, which I choose not to share. A hint: It begins with surgery and ends in Kansas City. I bet you wish. I wish, too.

By the way, I used to have a pitchfork just like the one you're holding to my throat. And I used to press the middle tine against the victim's Adam's apple. Is that a coincidence or what? You know, seeing as how we have so much in common, we should get together, a coffee date, just to see if we like each other, then dinner and a movie, a walk down the aisle, a couple of kids.

Won't it be funny, ten years from now, when we look back at what we'll laughingly refer to as *the pitchfork incident?*

## Tower of Babel

After I made love to the mannequin, I asked her if she
would like a cigarette. She chose not to respond. She was
aloof but striking with her shiny bald head, perfectly
melon-shaped. But it was her detachable torso that won me
over. I have always liked Northern European women. Cold,
yes, but with my fear of intimacy, what else could I ask for?
I remember telling this story to a doctor in Antarctica, who
couldn't quite fathom my meaning.

# Forgetting the Beast

I'm happy with the way things turned out. The sudden apoplexy of the family's best intentions, simmering on the back burner of grief, the side order of broken glass. Here is the end of the parable: *...and so it was determined. And so it was that the beast was unburdened and all the family felt another burden of guilt and shame relieved. And the beast, for lack of purpose, began to wander off through the open gate. Was it taken in or slaughtered? The family was too busy forgiving itself to care.*

# Trivia

There were two dogs running the ditch next to a country road. A car drove past and veered out of control. It struck a tree, a large sugar maple, the state tree of New York, and burst into flames.

Did I say two dogs? There were three, one of them a rare breed.

# Both Versions

In this version, the photograph emerges in twenty seconds
and is held between the fingers of a child. In the other
version, the photograph contains the child. It's fully devel-
oped—the photograph not the child—and reveals only
slightly what was on the child's mind. Whichever version
you prefer, there is a white border around the photograph.
It's the boundary between what happened—chemicalized
into stillness—and what continues to happen. In both
versions, the camera still holds the warmth of the hand that
snapped the picture. The slightest evidence that someone
loves the child.

# Perfect Beasts

*I understand all destructive urges.*
—Tom Verlaine

We were the origin of the species through the lens of a copulating pornographer. That cavalcade of leaves we piled into dramatic offerings, it didn't please the gods as much as we thought it would. How deep could that haze have been? I thought terms like "husband" and "wife" had become rather quaint. We kept trying to extricate ourselves but our bodies won out. The sex was... well, let's say we separated unnaturally from the rest of the world. In that respect, I still feel quite holy. The plum-ripe bruises on your thighs; the black and yellow haloes around your nipples. I dream of you as if you were never real. It was interesting, though, like a childbirth on TV. And how else would I know the monster of my mind if your monster hadn't asked? I think it's why I prefer to be alone, staring at perfect beasts. I will think of you always and never without seeds. Help. I think that's what I mean.

# Puppet Show Insurrection, Featuring a Brawl Between Punch and Judy

It made us laugh to see the stitched cloth rip at the seams, the motley dress discarded, as hands emerged from the bowels of the two who had only moments before been acting out their playful rage. So when the suddenly nude hands waved obscenely and reached blindly for each other, we thought it quaint, and the children laughed as though it were supposed to happen. Afterwards, a critic, who happened to be in attendance with his son, commented on the human tragedy and the esoteric nuances of the bald display of emotions. I simply wept to think the puppets weren't real.

## Cartoon Logic

To wake up content with dreaming as the room floats like a
square balloon or a really light and festive anvil.

# The Girl Who Loves Pork Rinds

She has all the boots you could ever imagine, all the strate-
gies of night. Her message is always clear in the way the sky
implies the weather. Her favorite dogs are dead. If she
murdered you and played in your remains, she'd hum
Waltzing Matilda to the deafness of your ear. The aisles are
full of women who covet ice cream and bars made of
chocolate, but the girl who loves pork rinds stands out
among them, her blonde hair dyed black, her wicked grin
disconcerting the butcher, who follows her with his eyes as
he wipes the beef blood on his apron. We are, all of us,
animals, tasting another day. There is meat enough for
bones to move, and the world spins slowly through space.
The riddle of who loves what is never solved. The grease
of things remains.

## Popular Song Used as Jingle, and the Resultant Love Affair

The song bored its way into his head without permission. He would not buy whatever it was. He would lie down and sleep the words of the song. He would dream the melody. There was a woman, but she could not understand the meaning. He slept. She moved around like yesterday, just out of sight. They were married in the moment when he woke to find her there, polishing the future with a rag she'd made from something old of his.

## Objectification Fascination

The breasts appeared in the fruit bowl on Friday, just before he found the buttocks in the freezer. The legs—long, with the calves at attention as if freshly shellacked while in high heels—were in the laundry basket. All of the pieces had the orangey sheen of fake tanning products. The faces were a bit disturbing. Especially the eyes. He would never look at a whole woman again, of that he was certain. Smaller, more manageable, he kept repeating.

## The Same Cow as Yesterday

Would you have me believe the cow that stands in that field is the same cow as yesterday, when I know that several of its kind are known to congregate there?

And what is your proof, besides the assertion of spots in places you remember?

Why do I spend my time with fools when I could easily invent a cure for thought and the diseases it breeds?

Let's ask the dog we killed last night, still wagging its infinite tail.

## Acknowledgements

Love and thanks to Mi for all her inspiration and editorial insights.

Thanks to Tobin O'Donnell for his thoughtful and intelligent edits, and to Brad Armstrong and Jeff Parker for all their good work on this book.

Thanks to Michael Burkard, Brian Evenson, Arthur Flowers, Mary Gaitskill, Bob Gates, Brooks Haxton, Mary Karr, Kevin Keck, Gary Lutz, George Saunders, Bruce Smith, and James Wagner for their support.

Thanks to Sharon Bedell, Mary Husak, and Terri Zollo for all their help over the years.

Thanks to the grad students in the creative writing program at Syracuse for all their kind words and enthusiasm.

As always, love and thanks to Steph Scheirer for her friendship and support.

Love and thanks to my brothers, Tim, Tom, and Jim, my sister, Ellen, and my mother.

And love to Tessa and Margeaux for teaching me much of what I know about how to love.